The
Active Reader

Book 1

Linda Kita-Bradley

Grass Roots Press

Edmonton, Alberta, Canada
2011

The Active Reader – Book 1 © 2011 Grass Roots Press

The Active Reader – Book 1 is published by

Grass Roots Press
A division of Literacy Services of Canada Ltd.
www.grassrootsbooks.net

AUTHOR	Linda Kita-Bradley
EDITOR	Pat Campbell
DESIGN	Lara Minja
LAYOUT	Susan Hunter

ACKNOWLEDGEMENTS

We acknowledge the financial support of the Government of Canada through the Book Publishing Industry Development Program (BPIDP) for our publishing activities.

We acknowledge the support of the Alberta Foundation for the Arts for our publishing programs.

ISBN 978-1-926583-15-0

Printed in Canada

Contents

About this workbook

Welcome to Book 1 of *The Active Reader* series. This workbook aims to engage learners in the process of active reading by providing reading passages and activities that help learners develop the skills and strategies to become fluent readers.

Reading Passage
Pre-reading questions introduce the passage and provide a purpose for reading.

The reading passage features high-frequency vocabulary and sight words, and repetitive text. Two post-reading questions encourage learners to think about the passage. The first question requires learners to make an inference. The second question requires learners to consider main ideas and details as they discuss the title of the passage.

Strategies

Word Family
After being introduced to a word family, learners are asked to (1) recognize words belonging to the word family in a short rhyme and (2) suggest more words that belong to the word family.

Letters and Sounds
Learners work through a set of activities that introduce target letter(s) and then reinforce letter-sound relationships.

Predict Words
Learners predict words by using meaning and/or print clues.

Assisted Reading
Learners read the passage with the educator's assistance. When the learners come across unfamiliar words, they are encouraged to use appropriate strategies.

Assisted Writing
Learners choose a topic and tell a story. The teacher serves as a scribe and writes down the learner's ideas.

Bike Ride

Letters:	R r and V v
Word Family:	an

- Look at the picture. What do you see?

- This is Roz.

  genai abap npoujouena

  Roz makes a car crash happen.

  How do you think

  Roz makes a car crash happen?

- Your teacher will read the story on page 2.

  Look at the words and pictures as your teacher reads.

  Find out how the car crash happens.

Bike Ride

Roz rides a bike to work.

Roz has to cross a road.

The road is very busy.

Roz waits at a crosswalk.

A van stops for Roz.

Roz can cross the road.

BOOM!

A car hits the van.

A lady gets out of the van.

A man gets out of the car.

Roz gives the lady her number.

Roz says, "Call me if you need a witness."

Roz gets a call a year later.

The call is from the lady.

The lady asks Roz to her wedding.

The lady says, "I want to thank you and your bike."

© BigStockPhoto/Paul Vorobyov

▶▶ Talk about the Story

1. Why do you think the lady thanks Roz and her bike?

2. The title of this story is **Bike Ride**.

   Explain how the title matches the story. Think of a new title.

Word Family

1. Say these words: can   man

   They belong to the **an** word family.

> A word family is a group of words that
>
> (1) sound the same and
> (2) have the same letter pattern.

2. Read the rhyme below with your teacher.

   Circle the words with the **an** letter pattern.

   A car hits a lady in a van.

   What good luck! She meets her man.

3. Read the words in the box with your teacher.

   Think of two more words in the **an** word family.

   Your teacher will print the words on the lines.

an

can

man

van

_____

_____

Letters and Sounds

1. Your teacher will read the words in the box.

   The words begin with the letter **r**.

   What sound does the letter **r** make?

   The letter **r** makes the sound /r/.

   Now read the words with your teacher.

Roz   road

ride

2. Think of three more words that begin with the sound /r/.

   Your teacher will print the words on the lines.

   ___ride___   ___read___   ___road___

3. What do you see in each picture?

   Say the word. Then say the first sound of the word.

   Does the word begin with the sound /r/? Circle yes or no.

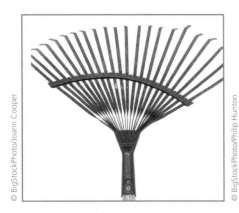

   (a) yes no   (b) yes no   (c) (yes) no

4. Your teacher will read the words in the box.

   The words begin with the letter **v**.

   What sound does the letter **v** make?

van	very

   The letter **v** makes the sound /v/.

   Now read the words with your teacher.

5. What do you see in each picture?

Say the word. Then say the first sound of the word.

Does the word begin with the sound /v/? Circle yes or no.

  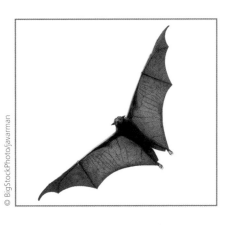

      (a) yes no   (b) yes no   (c) yes no

6. Your teacher will read the words in the box.

Listen. Circle the words that begin with the sound /v/.

wide	vote	voice

Predict Words

Your teacher will read each sentence on page 6.

Sound out the first letter of the missing word.

Say a word that makes sense. Your teacher will print the word.

1. Her favourite colour is r_e d,_____ .

2. He put the flowers in a v_a z o_._____ .

3. How much is the r_i v e_____ for this apartment?

4. Peas and carrots are my favourite v_e g e t a b l e s._ .

5. I use my r_i g h t_____ hand, not my left hand.

Assisted Reading

1. Read the story on page 2 again with your teacher.

2. Circle three words you want to learn. Copy the words into your dictionary.

Is a word hard to read?
Active readers use these strategies:

- Look for a letter pattern.
- Think of a word that makes sense.
- Sound out the letters they know.
- Ask someone for help.
- Skip the word.

Assisted Writing

1. Choose a topic from the box. Tell a story about it.

2. Watch your words turn into print. Your teacher will write down your story.

- How you met an important person in your life

- An accident that you witnessed

Just Stop!

Letters:	J j and K k
Word Family:	op

- Look at the picture. What do you see?

- This is Jan and her daughters.

  Jan has a cold. How do you think

  Jan gets over her cold?

- Your teacher will read the story on page 8.

  Look at the words and pictures as your teacher reads.

  Find out how Jan gets over her cold.

Just Stop!

Jan works all day.

She takes care of her kids.

She takes care of her home.

Jan does not stop. Jan gets a cold.

She feels tired.

She feels hot.

She has a sore throat.

Jan drinks tea and lemon.

She has hot soup.

But Jan does not rest.

She keeps going.

She works all day.

She takes care of her kids.

She takes care of her home.

Then Jan has to stop.

She just sleeps for two days.

And you know what?

Her kids help out at home.

Her boss says, "Stay home and rest."

Jan gets better.

▶▶ Talk about the Story

1. Do you think Jan will stay home from work the next time she is sick?

2. The title of this story is **Just Stop!**

Explain how the title matches the story. Think of a new title.

Word Family

1. Say these words: stop   hop

   They belong to the **op** word family.

> A word family is a group of words that
>
> (1) sound the same and
> (2) have the same letter pattern.

2. Read the rhyme below with your teacher.

   Circle the words with the **op** letter pattern.

   Jan just keeps going. She will not stop.

   She has to clean. She has to shop.

3. Read the words in the box with your teacher.

   Think of two more words in the **op** word family.

   Your teacher will print the words on the lines.

> **op**
>
> stop
>
> shop
>
> hop
>
> _____
>
> _____

Letters and Sounds

1. Your teacher will read the words in the box.

   The words begin with the letter **j**.

   What sound does the letter **j** make?

> Jan   just

   The letter j makes the sound /j/.

   Now read the words with your teacher.

2. What do you see in each picture?

   Say the word. Then say the first sound of the word.

   Does the word begin with the sound /j/? Circle yes or no.

(a) yes no   (b) (yes) no   (c) yes no

3. Your teacher will read the words in the box.

   Listen. Circle the words that begin with the sound /j/.

juice	jump	down

4. Your teacher will read the words in the box.

   The words begin with the letter **k**.

   What sound does the letter **k** make?

kids	keep

   The letter **k** makes the sound /k/.

   Now read the words with your teacher.

5. What do you see in each picture?

Say the word. Then say the first sound of the word.

Does the word begin with the sound /k/? Circle yes or no.

(b) yes no

(c) yes no

in the box.

begin with the sound /k/.

round

on page 12.

ssing word.

teacher will print the word.

JUST STOP!

1. I like peanut butter and j*uice* .

2. I put mustard and k*etchup* on my burger.

3. She likes to tell funny j*okes* !

4. Can you k*eep* a secret?

5. His birthday is in the month of J*uly.* .

Assisted Reading

1. Read the story on page 8 again with your teacher.

2. Circle three words you want to learn. Copy the words into your dictionary.

Is a word hard to read?
Active readers use these strategies:

- Look for a letter pattern.
- Think of a word that makes sense.
- Sound out the letters they know.
- Ask someone for help.
- Skip the word.

Assisted Writing

1. Choose a topic from the box. Tell a story about it.

2. Watch your words turn into print. Your teacher will write down your story.

- An event that made you really tired

- A time you helped somebody who was sick

UNIT 3 A Quick Meal

Letters: Qu qu and Z z

Word Family: it

- Look at the picture. What do you see?

- This is Zac.

  What do you think

  Zac is looking for?

- Your teacher will read the story on page 14.

  Look at the words and pictures as your teacher reads.

  Find out what Zac is looking for.

A Quick Meal

Zac is quite hungry.

He looks in the fridge.

Zac takes out meat.

He takes out mayo.

Zac makes a sandwich.

Zac puts his sandwich on the table.

Zac puts the meat in a Ziploc bag.

He puts the meat in the fridge.

He puts the mayo in the fridge.

Then Zac gets some milk.

Zac sits down to eat.

What! Zac's sandwich is gone!

Zac looks under the table.

He starts to laugh.

Zac pours his milk into his plate.

He puts the plate on the floor.

"Take the milk, too!" says Zac.

"Darn dog!"

▶▶ Talk about the Story

1. Why was the dog able to take Zac's sandwich?

2. The title of this story is **A Quick Meal**.

Explain how the title matches the story. Think of a new title.

Word Family

1. Say these words: sit   fit

   They belong to the **it** word family.

A word family is a group of words that

(1) sound the same and
(2) have the same letter pattern.

2. Read the rhyme below with your teacher.

   Circle the words with the **it** letter pattern.

   Zac's dog was fat, not fit.

   He always took food. He would not quit!

3. Read the words in the box with your teacher.

   Think of two more words in the **it** word family.

   Your teacher will print the words on the lines.

it

quit

sit

fit

_____

_____

Letters and Sounds

1. Your teacher will read the words in the box.

   The words begin with the letters **qu**.

   What sound do the letters **qu** make?

   quick   quite

   The letters **qu** make the sound /kw/.

   Now read the words with your teacher.

2. What do you see in each picture?

   Say the word. Then say the first sound of the word.

   Does the word begin with the sound /kw/? Circle yes or no.

   (a) (yes) no   (b) yes   no   (c) (yes) (no)

3. Your teacher will read the words in the box.

   Listen. Circle the words that begin with the sound /kw/.

   (quack)   build   quit

4. Your teacher will read the words in the box.

   The words begin with the letter **z**.

   What sound does the letter **z** make?

Zac	zip

   The letter **z** makes the sound /z/.

   Now read the words with your teacher.

5. What do you see in each picture?

Say the word. Then say the first sound of the word.

Does the word begin with the sound /z/? Circle yes or no.

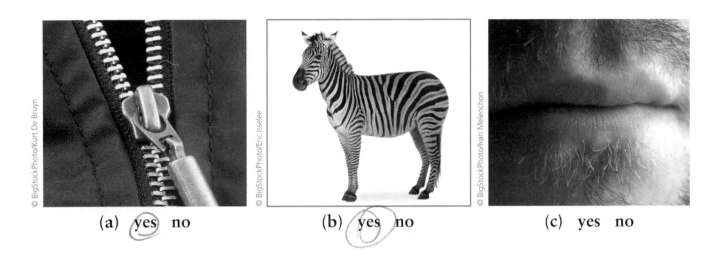

(a) yes no

(b) yes no

(c) yes no

6. Your teacher will read the words in the box.

Listen. Circle the words that begin with the sound /z/.

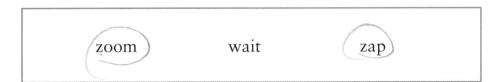

zoom   wait   zap

Predict Words

Your teacher will read each sentence on page 18.

Sound out the first letter(s) of the missing word.

Say a word that makes sense. Your teacher will print the word.

1. This is a library. Please be qu<u>iet</u> .

2. You can see wild animals in a z<u>oo</u> .

3. The king and qu<u>een</u> live in a palace.

4. One take away one equals z<u>ero</u> .

5. This is not a test. It is just a little qu<u>iz</u> .

Assisted Reading

1. Read the story on page 14 again with your teacher.

2. Circle three words you want to learn. Copy the words into your dictionary.

Is a word hard to read?
Active readers use these strategies:

- Look for a letter pattern.
- Think of a word that makes sense.
- Sound out the letters they know.
- Ask someone for help.
- Skip the word.

Assisted Writing

1. Choose a topic from the box. Tell a story about it.

2. Watch your words turn into print. Your teacher will write down your story.

- A favourite pet or animal story

- Something silly that made you laugh

Way too Tired!

Letters:	W w and X x
Word Family:	ook

- Look at the picture. What do you see?

- This is Max.

  Max works in a warehouse.

  What do you think

  Max does in the warehouse?

- Your teacher will read the story on page 20.

  Look at the words and pictures as your teacher reads.

  Find out what Max does in the warehouse.

Way Too Tired!

Max works in a warehouse.

Max puts books in boxes.

He gets the books ready to mail out.

Max cleans the warehouse, too.

He cleans the table.

He cleans the shelves.

He cleans the floor.

Max goes home.

He cooks supper. He eats.

Then Max cleans up.

He cleans the stove.

He cleans the sink.

At last Max can rest.

But Max just falls asleep.

He does not wash his face.

He does not brush his teeth.

Max has cleaned all day.

He is way too tired

to clean one more thing.

▶▶ Talk about the Story

1. Describe Max's day in your own words.

2. The title of this story is **Way Too Tired**!

Explain how the title matches the story. Think of a new title.

Word Family

1. Say these words: book took

   They belong to the **ook** word family.

A word family is a group of words that

(1) sound the same and
(2) have the same letter pattern.

2. Read the rhyme below with your teacher.

   Circle the words with the **ook** letter pattern.

   Max was tired. He could not look

   At one more box or one more book.

3. Read the words in the box with your teacher.

   Think of two more words in the **ook** word family.

   Your teacher will print the words on the lines.

ook

book

took

look

_____

_____

Letters and Sounds

1. Your teacher will read the words in the box.

   The words begin with the letter **w**.

   What sound does the letter **w** make?

   work   wash

   way

   The letter **w** makes the sound /w/.

   Now read the words with your teacher.

2. Think of three more words that begin with the sound /w/.

Your teacher will print the words on the lines.

__winers__   __walkaut__   __walk.__

3. What do you see in each picture?

Say the word. Then say the first sound of the word.

Does the word begin with the sound /w/? Circle yes or no.

(a) (yes) no   (b) (yes) no   (c) yes (no)

4. Your teacher will read the words in the box.

The words end with the letter **x**.

What sound does the letter **x** make?

The letter **x** makes the sound /ks/.

Now read the words with your teacher.

Max	box

5. What do you see in each picture?

Say the word. Does the word end with the sound /ks/?

Circle yes or no.

(a) yes no

(b) (yes) no

(c) (yes) no

6. Your teacher will read the words in the box.

Listen. Circle the words that end with the sound /ks/.

tax	few	fix

Predict Words

Your teacher will read each sentence on page 24.

Sound out the first letter(s) of the missing word.

Say a word that makes sense. Your teacher will print the word.

1. I want a drink of w<u>ater</u>.

2. Walking is a good way to ex<u>plorer</u>.

3. I am sick. I do not feel w<u>eel</u>.

4. The ex<u>piry</u> date tells you when food might go bad.

5. Washroom doors say Men or W<u>omem.</u>

Assisted Reading

1. Read the story on page 20 again with your teacher.

2. Circle three words you want to learn. Copy the words into your dictionary.

Is a word hard to read?
Active readers use these strategies:

- Look for a letter pattern.

- Think of a word that makes sense.

- Sound out the letters they know.

- Ask someone for help.

- Skip the word.

Assisted Writing

1. Choose a topic from the box. Tell a story about it.

2. Watch your words turn into print. Your teacher will write down your story.

- The worst thing you ever had to clean

- The first job you ever had

Cell Talk

Letter: C c

Word Family: ug

- Look at the picture. What do you see?

- This is Cindy and Ray.

  Ray is talking on his cell phone.

  How do you think Cindy feels?

- Your teacher will read the story on page 26.

  Look at the words and pictures as your teacher reads.

  Find out how Cindy feels.

Cell Talk

Cindy and Ray go for coffee.

Cindy's phone rings. She takes the call.

Cindy talks and talks.

Ray drinks his coffee.

Ray waits as Cindy talks.

Cindy stops talking.

She puts down her phone.

Ray's phone rings. He takes the call.

Ray talks and talks.

Cindy drinks her coffee.

Cindy waits as Ray talks.

Ray stops talking.

He puts down his phone.

Ray says, "Look at the time.

I have to go."

Ray gives Cindy a hug.

Cindy says, "It was good talking to you.

Let's go for coffee again."

Ray says, "Okay. I'll call you."

▶▶ Talk about the Story

1. Do you think Cindy and Ray are close friends?

2. The title of this story is **Cell Talk**.

Explain how the title matches the story. Think of a new title.

Word Family

1. Say these words: hug   dug

   They belong to the **ug** word family.

A word family is a group of words that

(1) sound the same and
(2) have the same letter pattern.

2. Read the rhyme below with your teacher.

   Circle the words with the **ug** letter pattern.

   Ray puts down his coffee mug.

   Ray gives Cindy a great big hug.

3. Read the words in the box with your teacher.

   Think of two more words in the **ug** word family.

   Your teacher will print the words on the lines.

ug

hug

dug

mug

_____

_____

Letters and Sounds

1. Your teacher will read the words in the box.

   The words begin with the letter **c**.

   What sound does the letter **c** make?

   The letter **c** makes the sound /k/.

   Now read the words with your teacher.

call   coffee

2. Your teacher will read the words in the box.

   The words begin with the letter **c**.

   What sound does the letter **c** make?

Cindy	cell

   The letter **c** makes the sound /s/.

   Now read the words with your teacher.

   The letter **c** makes two sounds.

   The /k/ sound is called hard c.

   The /s/ sound is called soft c.

   When **c** is followed by **e, i** or **y**,

   it makes the soft sound /s/.

3. What do you see in each picture?

   Say the word. Then say the first sound of the word.

   Does the word begin with hard c, /k/, or soft c, /s/?

   Circle /k/ or /s/.

   (a) /k/ /s/   (b) /k/ /s/   (c) /k/ /s/

BigStockPhoto/Jessica Morrow

(d) /k/ /s/

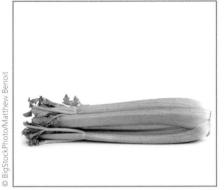

BigStockPhoto/Matthew Benoit

(e) /k/ /s/

BigStockPhoto/Elke Dennis

(f) /k/ /s/

4. Your teacher will read the words in the box.

Listen. Circle the words that begin with hard c, /k/.

ceiling	cab	could	city
come	cold	certain	came

Predict Words

Your teacher will read each sentence on page 30.

Sound out the first letter of the missing word.

Say a word that makes sense. Your teacher will print the word.

HINT: The letter c makes two sounds: hard c and soft c.

1. Red is my favourite c _olor,_ .

2. I have a brush and c _ellphone_ in my purse.

3. Put the food in the shopping c _entre,_ .

4. The pay phone costs 50 c _ent,_ .

5. I do not like to be the c _entre,_ of attention.

Assisted Reading

1. Read the story on page 26 again with your teacher.

2. Circle three words you want to learn. Copy the words into your dictionary.

> Is a word hard to read?
> Active readers use these strategies:
>
> - Look for a letter pattern.
> - Think of a word that makes sense.
> - Sound out the letters they know.
> - Ask someone for help.
> - Skip the word.

Assisted Writing

1. Choose a topic from the box. Tell a story about it.

2. Watch your words turn into print. Your teacher will write down your story.

- A time you used your cell in an emergency

- A friend you have fun with

Good Time, Bad Time

Letter:	G g
Word Family:	et

- Look at the picture. What do you see?

- This is Gina. She is sick.

  Gina drank too much.

  Why do you think

  Gina drank too much?

- Your teacher will read the story on page 32.

  Look at the words and pictures as your teacher reads.

  Find out why Gina drank too much.

Good Time, Bad Time

Gina is at a party.

Gina is shy. No one talks to her.

So Gina has a beer.

Now Gina is less shy.

She starts to talk.

Gina has one more beer.

Then Gina has one beer too many.

Gina is sick the next day.

Her head hurts. Her stomach is upset.

Gina wants to get better.

Gina drinks tea. She still feels sick.

Gina drinks ginger ale. She still feels sick.

Gina drinks milk. She still feels sick.

Gina drinks water. She still feels sick.

Gina calls a friend.

Gina says, "I still feel sick."

Gina's friend says, "Drink less."

▶▶ Talk about the Story

1. Do you think Gina will listen to her friend?

2. The title of this story is **Good Time, Bad Time**.

Explain how the title matches the story. Think of a new title.

Word Family

1. Say these words: set   get

   They belong to the **et** word family.

A word family is a group of words that

(1) sound the same and
(2) have the same letter pattern.

2. Read the rhyme below with your teacher.

   Circle the words with the **et** letter pattern.

   Gina's stomach was upset.

   Does she feel better? No, not yet.

3. Read the words in the box with your teacher.

   Think of two more words in the **et** word family.

   Your teacher will print the words on the lines.

et

upset

get

yet

_____

_____

Letters and Sounds

1. Your teacher will read the words in the box.

   The words begin with the letter **g**.

   What sound does the letter **g** make?

good   go

   The letter **g** makes the sound /g/.

   Now read the words with your teacher.

2. Your teacher will read the words in the box.

   The words begin with the letter **g**.

   What sound does the letter **g** make?

Gina   ginger

   The letter **g** makes the sound /j/.

   Now read the words with your teacher.

   The letter **g** makes two sounds.

   The /g/ sound is called hard g.

   The /j/ sound is called soft g.

When **g** is followed by **e**, **i** or **y**, it often makes the soft sound /j/.

3. What do you see in each picture?

   Say the word. Then say the first sound of the word.

   Does the word begin with hard g, /g/, or soft g, /j/?

   Circle /g/ or /j/.

(a) /g/ /j/   (b) /g/ /j/   (c) /g/ /j/

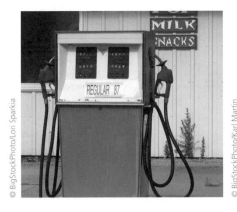

(d) /g/ /j/   (e) /g/ /j/   (f) /g/ /j/

4. Your teacher will read the words in the box.

Listen. Circle the words that begin with hard g, /g/.

gone	gem	gift	gum
gold	gin	guy	gym

Predict Words

Your teacher will read each sentence on page 36.

Sound out the first letter of the missing word.

Say a word that makes sense. Your teacher will print the word.

HINT: The letter g makes two sounds: hard g and soft g.

1. I have one boy and two g _____ .

2. I do not know the answer. I will have to g _____ .

3. Can I g _____ you some advice?

4. Wash your hands. Don't spread g _____ .

5. My dad is a big man. He is as big as a g _____ .

Assisted Reading

1. Read the story on page 32 again
   with your teacher.

2. Circle three words you want to learn.
   Copy the words into your dictionary.

Is a word hard to read?
Active readers use these strategies:

- Look for a letter pattern.

- Think of a word that makes sense.

- Sound out the letters they know.

- Ask someone for help.

- Skip the word.

Assisted Writing

1. Choose a topic from the box.
   Tell a story about it.

2. Watch your words turn into print.
   Your teacher will write down your story.

- A time you felt shy

- Something you regret
  doing or saying

A Lucky Man

Letter:	Short A a
Word Family:	ad

- Look at the picture. What do you see?

- This is Monty.

  Monty has a new job.

  What do you think

  Monty's new job is?

- Your teacher will read the story on page 38.

  Look at the words and pictures as your teacher reads.

  Find out about Monty's new job.

A Lucky Man

Monty used to work a crane.
Monty sat in the cab all day.
Monty saw people pass by.
He liked to wave to the people.

One day some men robbed Monty.
The men beat up Monty really bad.
Monty had to quit his job.

Now Monty hands out papers.
Monty waves to people.
Monty talks to people.
Monty makes people smile.

Monty hands out more than papers.
Monty keeps food in a box on his chair.
Monty gives food to homeless people.

Monty says, "This job is low pay.
But it is the best job I ever had."

© BigStockPhoto/Viacheslav Zotov

▶▶ Talk about the Story

1. Why do you think Monty had to quit his job on the crane?

2. The title of this story is **A Lucky Man**.

Explain how the title matches the story. Think of a new title.

Word Family

1. Say these words: bad   had

   They belong to the **ad** word family.

> A word family is a group of words that
>
> (1) sound the same and
> (2) have the same letter pattern.

2. Read the rhyme below with your teacher.

   Circle the words with the **ad** letter pattern.

      Some of Monty's luck was bad.

      But Monty does not like to feel sad.

3. Read the words in the box with your teacher.

   Think of two more words in the **ad** word family.

   Your teacher will print the words on the lines.

> **ad**
>
> bad
>
> had
>
> sad
>
> _____
>
> _____

Letters and Sounds

1. Say these words: sat   cab   pass

   They have the short sound /a/.

   The letter **a** makes the short sound /a/.

2. Your teacher will read the words below.

   Listen. Circle the words that have the short sound /a/.

   back   make   man

Predict Words

Your teacher will read each sentence.

Fill in the missing word. Your teacher will print the word.

You can use any word that makes sense.

1. It is cold. Put a _____ on your head.

2. I hear water dripping. Did you turn off the _____ ?

3. How long did the movie _____ ?

Assisted Reading

1. Read the story on page 38 again with your teacher.

2. Circle three words you want to learn. Copy the words into your dictionary.

Is a word hard to read?
Active readers use these strategies:

- Look for a letter pattern.
- Think of a word that makes sense.
- Sound out the letters they know.
- Ask someone for help.
- Skip the word.

Assisted Writing

1. Choose a topic from the box. Tell a story about it.

2. Watch your words turn into print. Your teacher will write down your story.

- The best job you ever had

- A time you had to quit something

Bedtime Blues

Letter:	Short E e
Word Family:	at

- Look at the picture. What do you see?

- This is Pat.

    Pat looks mad.

    Why do you think

    Pat looks mad?

- Your teacher will read the story on page 42.

    Look at the words and pictures as your teacher reads.

    Find out why Pat looks mad.

Bedtime Blues

Les is late.

Pat is mad.

Les does not want to fight.

Les goes to bed.

Pat goes to bed.

Pat is still mad.

She does not sleep.

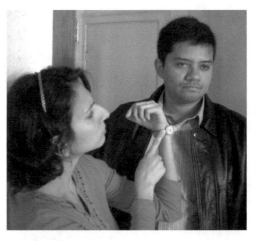

The next day Pat is still mad.

Les is nice to Pat all day.

Les makes Pat a cup of tea.

But Pat does not talk to him.

Les feels bad.

Les says, "Please talk to me."

Pat and Les talk.

Pat says, "I worry.

I worry when you are late."

That night Les stays home.

Pat and Les go to bed.

Pat feels better.

And so does Les.

▶▶ Talk about the Story

1. Why do you think Pat and Les feel better?

2. The title of this story is **Bedtime Blues**.

Explain how the title matches the story. Think of a new title.

Word Family

1. Say these words: **Pat   that**

   They belong to the **at** word family.

A word family is a group of words that

(1) sound the same and
(2) have the same letter pattern.

2. Read the rhyme below with your teacher.

   Circle the words with the **at** letter pattern.

   Pat thinks Les is a rat.

   And that is that!

3. Read the words in the box with your teacher.

   Think of two more words in the **at** word family.

   Your teacher will print the words on the lines.

at

Pat

that

rat

_____

_____

Letters and Sounds

1. Say these words: **Les   next   bed**

   They have the short sound /e/.

   The letter **e** makes the short sound /e/.

2. Your teacher will read the words below.

   Listen. Circle the words that have the short sound /e/.

   let   tell   please

Predict Words

Your teacher will read each sentence.

Fill in the missing word. Your teacher will print the word.

You can use any word that makes sense.

1. He passed his math _____ .

2. There is a leak. The floor is all _____ .

3. My _____ get sore when I run up a hill.

Assisted Reading

1. Read the story on page 42 again with your teacher.

2. Circle three words you want to learn. Copy the words into your dictionary.

Is a word hard to read?
Active readers use these strategies:

- Look for a letter pattern.

- Think of a word that makes sense.

- Sound out the letters they know.

- Ask someone for help.

- Skip the word.

Assisted Writing

1. Choose a topic from the box. Tell a story about it.

2. Watch your words turn into print. Your teacher will write down your story.

- A time you worried about somebody

- A time you could not fall asleep

The Boss

Letter:	Short O o
Word Family:	ot

- Look at the picture. What do you see?

- This is Dot.

  Dot lives on her own.

  Why do you think

  Dot likes to live on her own?

- Your teacher will read the story on page 46.

  Look at the words and pictures as your teacher reads.

  Find out why Dot likes to live on her own.

The Boss

Dot lives on her own.
She is the boss in her home.
Dot can watch TV when she wants.
She can listen to music when she wants.
She can go to bed early when she wants.

Dot has a dog.
The dog's name is Mugs.
Mugs barks at the TV.
Mugs barks at the music.
Mugs barks when Dot goes to bed early.

So, Dot does not go to bed early.
She takes Mugs for a walk.
Dot does not listen to music.
She plays ball with Mugs.
Dot does not watch TV.
She plays fetch with Mugs.
Lucky Mugs!

▶▶ Talk about the Story

1. Why do you think Mugs is lucky?

2. The title of this story is **The Boss**.

Explain how the title matches the story. Think of a new title.

Word Family

1. Say these words: Dot   not

   They belong to the **ot** word family.

> A word family is a group of words that
>
> (1) sound the same and
> (2) have the same letter pattern.

2. Read the rhyme below with your teacher.

   Circle the words with the **ot** letter pattern.

   Dot thinks she's the boss. But she's not.

   Dot must play with Mugs a lot.

3. Read the words in the box with your teacher.

   Think of two more words in the **ot** word family.

   Your teacher will print the words on the lines.

ot
Dot
not
lot
_____
_____

Letters and Sounds

1. Say these words: dog   boss

   They have the short sound /o/.

   The letter **o** makes the short sound /o/.

2. Your teacher will read the words below.

   Listen. Circle the words that have the short sound /o/.

job	box	home

Predict Words

Your teacher will read each sentence.

Fill in the missing word. Your teacher will print the word.

You can use any word that makes sense.

1. I wait at the same bus _____ each day.

2. I do not like to _____ for clothes.

3. Let's go. Did you _____ the door?

Assisted Reading

1. Read the story on page 46 again with your teacher.

2. Circle three words you want to learn. Copy the words into your dictionary.

Is a word hard to read?
Active readers use these strategies:

- Look for a letter pattern.

- Think of a word that makes sense.

- Sound out the letters they know.

- Ask someone for help.

- Skip the word.

Assisted Writing

1. Choose a topic from the box. Tell a story about it.

2. Watch your words turn into print. Your teacher will write down your story.

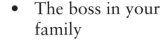

- The boss in your family

- Your favourite person to live with

His Dreams

| **Letter:** | Short I i |
| **Word Family:** | all |

- Look at the picture. What do you see?

© BigStockPhoto/Suzanne Tucker

- This is Jim.

  Jim works in a mall.

  How do you think Jim feels about his job?

- Your teacher will read the story on page 50.

  Look at the words and pictures as your teacher reads.

  Find out how Jim feels about his job.

His Dreams

Jim works in a mall.
Jim cleans floors.
He does not like to clean floors.
Jim says, "Cleaning floors
is women's work."

But Jim cannot get other work.
Jim tries to learn English.
Jim tries to get his high school.
But he has no time.
He has no money.

The years go by.
Jim has four kids.
Jim works for his kids.
His kids go to college.
His kids have a good life.

Jim still works in a mall.
He cleans floors.
Jim dreams of a farm.
Jim dreams of a farm
he will never have.

▶▶ Talk about the Story

1. How do you think Jim feels about his life?

2. The title of this story is **His Dreams**.

Explain how the title matches the story. Think of a new title.

Word Family

1. Say these words: mall   tall

   They belong to the **all** word family.

2. Read the rhyme below with your teacher.

   Circle the words with the **all** letter pattern.

   My job can make me feel small.

   But my kids make me walk tall.

3. Read the words in the box with your teacher.

   Think of two more words in the **all** word family.

   Your teacher will print the words on the lines.

all

small

tall

mall

_____

_____

Letters and Sounds

1. Say these words: Jim   his   kid

   They have the short sound /i/.

   The letter **i** makes the short sound /i/.

2. Your teacher will read the words below.

   Listen. Circle the words that have the short sound /i/.

   miss   time   fill

Predict Words

Your teacher will read each sentence.

Fill in the missing word. Your teacher will print the word.

You can use any word that makes sense.

1. Here is a chair. Please _____ down.

2. I ate something bad. Now I feel _____ .

3. I need a small car, not a _____ car.

Assisted Reading

1. Read the story on page 50 again
   with your teacher.

2. Circle three words you want to learn.
   Copy the words into your dictionary.

Is a word hard to read?
Active readers use these strategies:

- Look for a letter pattern.
- Think of a word that makes sense.
- Sound out the letters they know.
- Ask someone for help.
- Skip the word.

Assisted Writing

1. Choose a topic from the box.
   Tell a story about it.

2. Watch your words turn into print.
   Your teacher will write down your story.

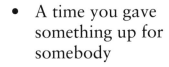

- A time you gave
  something up for
  somebody

- A time somebody gave up
  something for you

Up in Smoke?

Letter:	Short U u
Word Family:	ap

- Look at the picture. What do you see?

- This is Liz.

  What do you think

  Liz is doing?

- Your teacher will read the story on page 54.

  Look at the words and pictures as your teacher reads.

  Find out what Liz is doing.

Up in Smoke?

Liz is cooking.
Liz is cooking with oil.
The oil is too hot.
The oil gives off smoke.
The smoke alarm goes off.
Liz jumps! The alarm is so loud!

Liz gets a dishtowel.
She waves the towel near the alarm.
The smoke clears. The alarm stops.
Liz starts to cook again.
But the alarm goes off again.
Liz gets on a chair.
She shuts off the alarm.

Liz is done cooking.
Liz lights a candle. She eats.
Then Liz has a nap.

The candle burns.
And the smoke alarm?
It is still shut off.

▶▶ Talk about the Story

1. Describe Liz in your own words.

2. The title of this story is **Up in Smoke?**

Explain how the title matches the story. Think of a new title.

Word Family

1. Say these words: nap cap

   They belong to the **ap** word family.

> A word family is a group of words that
>
> (1) sound the same and
> (2) have the same letter pattern.

2. Read the rhyme below with your teacher.

   Circle the words with the **ap** letter pattern.

   Liz lights a candle. Liz has a nap.

   Good thing her home is not a fire trap.

3. Read the words in the box with your teacher.

   Think of two more words in the **ap** word family.

   Your teacher will print the words on the lines.

ap

trap

nap

cap

_____

_____

Letters and Sounds

1. Say these words: but up shut

   They have the short sound /u/.

   The letter **u** makes the short sound /u/.

2. Your teacher will read the words below.

   Listen. Circle the words that have the short sound /u/.

   such   luck   use

Predict Words

Your teacher will read each sentence.

Fill in the missing word. Your teacher will print the word.

You can use any word that makes sense.

1. She poured the tea into the _____ .

2. Be careful with that knife. Don't _____ yourself.

3. Take some back. You gave me too _____ .

Assisted Reading

1. Read the story on page 54 again with your teacher.

2. Circle three words you want to learn. Copy the words into your dictionary.

> Is a word hard to read?
> Active readers use these strategies:
>
> - Look for a letter pattern.
> - Think of a word that makes sense.
> - Sound out the letters they know.
> - Ask someone for help.
> - Skip the word.

Assisted Writing

1. Choose a topic from the box. Tell a story about it.

2. Watch your words turn into print. Your teacher will write down your story.

- A time you did something that was not safe

- A time you had good luck

I Miss You

Letter:	Y y
Word Family:	in

- Look at the picture. What do you see?

- Describe this family in your own words.

- Your teacher will read the story on page 58.

  Look at the words and pictures as your teacher reads.

  Find out more about this family.

I Miss You

My dad and I are friends.
We talk every day.
We cook meals.
We play cards.
Or we just sit.
We do not have to talk.
We are happy to be with each other.

I get a call one day.
My dad died. Just like that.
My dad died in his sleep.

I have a son. His name is Vin.
Vin is still young.
Vin still needs a mom,
not a friend.
But I know one thing for sure.
I know Vin will grow up.
Vin will grow up to be my friend.

Thank you, Dad.

▶▶ Talk about the Story

1. Why do you think the writer thanks her dad?

2. The title of this story is **I Miss You**.

Explain how the title matches the story. Think of a new title.

Word Family

1. Say these words: Vin   tin

   They belong to the **in** word family.

> A word family is a group of words that
>
> (1) sound the same and
> (2) have the same letter pattern.

2. Read the rhyme below with your teacher.

   Circle the words with the **in** letter pattern.

   I play cards with Vin.

   Vin never loses. I never win.

in
Vin
tin
win
_____
_____

3. Read the words in the box with your teacher.

   Think of two more words in the **in** word family.

   Your teacher will print the words on the lines.

Letters and Sounds

1. Say these words: you   young

   They begin with the sound /y/.

   The letter **y** makes the sound /y/.

2. Your teacher will read the words below.

   Listen. Circle the words that begin with the sound /y/.

yes	wet	your

Predict Words

Your teacher will read each sentence.

Sound out the first letter of the missing word.

Say a word that makes sense. Your teacher will print the word.

1. His favourite colour is y_____ .

2. She is 32 y_____ old.

3. I can hear you. You do not have to y_____ .

Assisted Reading

1. Read the story on page 58 again with your teacher.

2. Circle three words you want to learn. Copy the words into your dictionary.

Is a word hard to read?
Active readers use these strategies:

- Look for a letter pattern.

- Think of a word that makes sense.

- Sound out the letters they know.

- Ask someone for help.

- Skip the word.

Assisted Writing

1. Choose a topic from the box. Tell a story about it.

2. Watch your words turn into print. Your teacher will write down your story.

- A memory you have about somebody you loved

- The last time you spent time with a good friend

ANSWER KEY

In some cases, the answer key contains only a few of the possible responses for questions. There are other acceptable responses for these questions.

Unit 1: Bike Ride

Talk About the Story: 1. If the lady had not stopped for Roz, she would not have met her husband. **2.** Possible response: Roz's bike ride was very important in the lady's life.

Word Family: 2. van, man **3.** Possible responses: ban, Dan, fan, Nan, pan, plan, ran, tan, Stan

Letters and Sounds: 3a. yes: rake **3b.** no: logs **3c.** yes: race, run **5a.** yes: vacuum **5b.** yes: volcano **5c.** no: bat **6.** vote, voice

Predict Words: 1. red **2.** vase **3.** rent **4.** vegetable **5.** right

Unit 2: Just Stop!

Talk About the Story: 1. Possible responses: No. Jill has to go to work so she can support her kids. Yes. Jill knows her boss wants her to stay home when she is sick. **2.** Possible response: The only way Jill got better was just to stop and sleep for two days.

Word Family: 2. stop, shop **3.** Possible responses: bop, cop, drop, mop, pop, top

Letters and Sounds: 2a. no: bells **2b.** yes: jewellery box **2c.** yes: judge **3.** juice, jump **5a.** no: hats **5b.** yes: keys **5c.** yes: kite **6.** kind, kiss

Predict Words: 1. jam; jelly **2.** ketchup **3.** jokes **4.** keep **5.** June; July; January

Unit 3: A Quick Meal

Talk About the Story: 1. Zac was not paying attention to the dog because he was busy in the kitchen. **2.** Possible responses: Zac made himself a sandwich, which is a quick meal. The dog got a quick meal because he took Zac's sandwich.

Word Family: 2. fit, quit **3.** Possible responses: bit, grit, hit, kit, knit, lit, pit, wit, zit

Letters and Sounds: 2a. yes: question mark **2b.** no: whale **2c.** yes: quarter **3.** quack, quit **5a.** yes: zipper **5b.** yes: zebra **5c.** no: mouth **6.** zoom, zap

Predict Words: 1. quiet **2.** zoo **3.** queen **4.** zero **5.** quiz

Unit 4: Way Too Tired!

Talk About the Story: 1. Possible responses: busy, full of cleaning, routine, tiring **2.** Possible responses: Max is so tired he falls asleep on the couch. Max is so tired he will just go to bed without washing.

Word Family: 2. look, book **3.** Possible responses: cook, hook, shook

Letters and Sounds: 3a. yes: window **3b.** yes: watch **3c.** no: pot **5a.** no: boat **5b.** yes: fox **5c.** yes: six **6.** tax, fix

Predict Words: 1. water; wine **2.** exercise **3.** well **4.** expiry **5.** Women

Unit 5: Cell Talk

Talk About the Story: 1. Possible responses: Yes. They like to get together for coffee. They give each other hugs. No. They are more interested in talking on their cell phones than to each other. **2.** Possible response: Cindy and Ray talk on their cell phones a lot, not to each other.

Word Family: 2. mug, hug **3.** Possible responses: bug, jug, lug, plug, rug, slug, tug

Letters and Sounds: 3a. /k/: car **3b.** /s/: cigarettes **3c.** /s/: cereal **3d.** /k/: cans **3e.** /s/: celery **3f.** /k/: cake **4.** cab, could, come, cold, came

Predict Words: 1. colour **2.** comb **3.** cart **4.** cents **5.** centre

Unit 6: Good Time, Bad Time

Talk About the Story: 1. Possible responses: No. Gina is shy so she drinks to feel more relaxed around people. Gina might try to take her friend's advice but it will be hard for her. **2.** Possible responses: At first Gina has a bad time at the party because she is shy, but she starts to have a good time when she has a drink. Gina relaxes and has a good time when she drinks, but the next day is a bad time because she is sick.

Word Family: 2. upset, yet **3.** Possible responses: bet, jet, let, met, net, pet, set, vet, wet

Letters and Sounds: 3a. /g/: garbage cans **3b.** /g/: guitar **3c.** /j/: giraffe **3d.** /g/: gas **3e.** /g/: gun **3f.** /g/: ghost **4.** gone, gift, gum, gold, guy (Note: The soft/hard g rule has a 64 percent reliability. Common words that are exceptions are get, gift, girl, and give.)

Predict Words: 1. girls **2.** guess **3.** give **4.** germs **5.** giant

Unit 7: A Lucky Man

Talk About the Story: 1. Possible responses: Monty was too hurt to work after the men beat him up. Monty had a bad back from the beating, so he could not work the crane all day. **2.** Monty was unlucky because he had to quit his old job. But he is lucky now because he has a job that gives him a chance to be with people.

Word Family: 2. bad, sad **3.** Possible responses: dad, fad, glad, lad, mad, pad, tad

Letters and Sounds: 2. back, man

Predict Words: 1. hat, cap **2.** tap, faucet, water **3.** last

Unit 8: Bedtime Blues

Talk About the Story: 1. Possible response: Pat and Les feel better because they talked things over with each other. **2.** Possible response: When you have the blues, it means you feel sad. Bedtime was a sad time for Pat when she was mad at Les.

Word Family: 2. Pat, rat, that **3.** Possible responses: bat, cat, fat, hat, mat, sat, vat

Letters and Sounds: 2. let, tell

Predict Words: 1. test, quiz **2.** wet **3.** legs, back

Unit 9: The Boss

Talk About the Story: 1. Possible responses: Dot puts Mugs first. Dot plays with Mugs and walks him instead of doing what she wants. **2.** Dot thinks she is the boss, but Mugs is really the boss.

Word Family: 2. Dot, lot, not **3.** Possible responses: cot, got, jot, pot, rot, tot

Letters and Sounds: 2. job, box

Predict Words: 1. stop, station **2.** shop, look **3.** lock

Unit 10: His Dreams

Talk About the Story: 1. Possible responses: Jim feels let down because he could not get a better job, improve his English, or have a farm. Jim feels happy because he helped his kids get a good life. **2.** Possible response: Jim had dreams of getting a better job, improving his English, having a farm, and giving his kids a good life.

Word Family: 2. small, tall **3.** Possible responses: ball, call, fall, gall, hall, stall, wall

Letters and Sounds: 2. miss, fill

Predict Words: 1. sit **2.** sick, ill, bad **3.** big

Unit 11: Up in Smoke?

Talk About the Story: 1. Possible responses: Liz is careless. Liz takes chances. Liz is lucky (that a fire has not started). **2.** Possible response: Go up in smoke means to start on fire. Liz's home might go up in smoke because Liz left the candle burning, and she forgot to reset the smoke alarm.

Word Family: 2. nap, trap **3.** Possible responses: clap, flap, gap, lap, map, pap, rap, sap, slap, strap, tap, whap, yap, zap

Letters and Sounds: 2. such, luck

Predict Words: 1. cup, mug **2.** cut, hurt **3.** much

Unit 12: I Miss You

Talk About the Story: 1. The writer learned how to raise kids from the way her dad raised her.
2. Possible responses: The writer misses spending time with her dad. The writer thinks about her dad and wants him to know that she misses him.

Word Family: 2. Vin, win **3.** Possible responses: bin, chin, din, gin, pin, sin, spin, thin

Letters and Sounds: 2. yes, your

Predict Words: 1. yellow **2.** years **3.** yell